THANK GOD
I Don't Look Like What I've Been Through

Psalm 18:2 - The LORD is my rock and my fortress and my deliverer, my God, my rock, in whom I take refuge, my shield, and the horn of my salvation, my strong hold.

Elder Crystal Varner, MBA

Copyright © 2016 Crystal Varner

All rights reserved.

ISBN-13: **978-0692624128**
ISBN-10: **0692624120**

DEDICATION

I thank God, My Lord and Savior for giving me an avenue to share His word with the world. You used me as the vessel to live through the trials only to get your message out. I will forever be grateful that You were mindful of me.

CONTENTS

ACKNOWLEDGMENTS i

1	MY PROTECTOR	9-23
2	MY KEEPER	24-40
3	MY SAVIOR	41-53
4	MY PROVIDER	54-66
5	MY WAYMAKER	67-76
6	MY DELIVERER	77-90
7	TRANSFORMATION	91-97
8	MY RESTORER	98-110
9	LOVER OF MY SOUL	111-120
10	SEASON OF SEPERATION	121-130
11	WORDS OF ENCOURAGEMENT	131-133

ACKNOWLEDGMENTS

HOLY SPIRIT – THANK YOU!

To my husband, my rock! Thank you for being supportive, patient and loving me in spite of my shortcomings. You taught me how to be a better woman and to love you how God intended.

To my Pastor and First Lady, De'Juan and Stacey Kelker – as always, thank you for your continuous love, support and prayers. Thank you for being obedient to the calling and speaking, teaching and preaching the messages that God entrusted you with. May God continue to be the anchor of your lives.

INTRODUCTION

Growing up, I never really understood the feeling of abandonment that I often experienced. I lived in a house with 6 other siblings, our mother and multiple family members. There was a lot of love between us all, and even though we rarely heard the words "I love you" it was an unspoken truth in our family.

As I grew older, I often heard the phrase – "you weren't created to fit in, but stand out." But how do you stand out when you have no idea who you are? I don't remember anyone ever asking me what I wanted to be when I grew up. It wasn't because they didn't care – because I know they did...they were just busy.

Mom worked two jobs to take care of 7 kids...and dad; well he had two families and he didn't live with ours. And quite frankly, he wasn't a very emotional man...no fault of his own. Maybe that's how he was raised. All I know is that I needed love, and even though it was an unspoken truth – I wanted so much more. So when Mr. Wrong and the wrong Mr. Right told me they loved me, I believed them. I had never seen a "real relationship" based off of love in our home, so I wasn't conditioned to identify a counterfeit.

My brother's best friend – counterfeit! Mr. Wrong a.k.a. my first love – counterfeit! Mr. Right a.k.a. Mr. Wrong #2 a.k.a. baby daddy of all 4 children – counterfeit! GOD…the real deal. When HE began to show me that I was fearfully and wonderfully made…I began to understand the saying, "praise HIM on the mountain top and praise HIM in the valley." I didn't fit in and that was okay. And with every test and trial, I found a reason to praise HIM.

CHAPTER 1 – MY PROTECTOR

Biblical meaning of numbers:

8: A new beginning. After God created the earth everything was a new.

7: The number of completeness and perfection (both physical and spiritual). God created the earth in 6 days and on the 7th day He blessed it and rested.

19: Faith.

6 symbolizes: Man and human weakness; manifestation of sin.

7: The number of completeness and perfection (both physical and spiritual).

I was born 8/7/1967...and the biblical numeric meaning is a good picture of my life from the beginning until now. I was given a new beginning after God stepped in and said enough is enough and completed the work He had begun. But first I had to experience weakness at what I call the lowest points in my life; because of the continuous sin that I chose to live in. But through it all, I somehow had faith as a mustard seed and with every trial, God showed Himself to be true and my faith increased. He changed me physically and spiritually, completed me and restored.

Growing up with six other siblings, there were always people around and things to do. Our house was the house on the block that everyone flocked to with people constantly coming and going, sort of like a revolving door at times. With so many kids in the home, we always had something to do. I remember our summers were spent playing hide-n-go-seek, tag, kickball, hopscotch, double-dutch and planning talent shows in the backyard. And because I was the youngest girl, I was rarely allowed to participate in the talent shows. Every weekend my siblings and one of the neighbor boys pretended to be Sister Sledge, Emotions and the Sylver's; as they charged the other neighbor kids $.25 each to come to the show in the backyard or they could look over the fence for free.

Fall was spent "borrowing" shopping carts from the grocery stores because we needed them for our haunted houses that we built in the basement every year. We would section off rooms with curtains or blankets, put our friends in the carts and race them from room to room in the basement, as my siblings or one of their friends would jump out from behind the curtains and scare them. All for a small fee of $.50 each.

Winters were just as exciting as summer and fall. We would either toboggan down the hill behind Bob's Hamburg, ice skate down the middle of our street, have snowball fights while using socks as mittens, because with seven children in the house, we could never keep track of our gloves. Or we would tare cardboard into enough pieces for us all to have a section and drag each other down the ice covered street. I have a lot of great memories…sweet, sweet memories. But there is one memory that has lain dormant in the back of my mind for years.

Growing up in our home was fun but I was different than my sisters. I was flat chested, had big lips, big nose and I looked more like my father than I did my sisters. And for some reason I always felt inferior; like an outcast, but never knew why. Being called ugly, even if it was just a joke, made me feel less than my siblings. Why was I so different? Why did I not fit in? My only dream as a little girl was to be like my older sisters, fun loving, outgoing and to have boobs and a butt. But instead, at the age of 11 when most girls were beginning to blossom, I was 5'5", 100lbs soaking wet and pencil thin. It was apparent that, no matter what I did, how much toilet paper I stuffed to try to look like them, I wasn't them.

I was a carefree girl. Didn't really run after

boys, because my mom taught us girls better. Plus if she knew I had a boyfriend, I would have gotten the snot beat out of me. So when different neighborhood boys and my brother's friends visited the house, it didn't excite me because I knew they were off limits. My brother's best friend was always at our house. He didn't live far – maybe 3 blocks in walking distance. I believe that he was starting to like one of my sisters – but she was already dating one of the neighborhood boys from across the street. My brother's friend was extremely tall, uncoordinated and clumsy, bucked teeth and unattractive. We thought he was weird, but we had all become used to his "weirdness". Heck, he had been around our family for so long, that he was practically one of us. He was a giant compared to me, standing about 6'7" tall.

One day my brother's friend asked me to walk to the store with him and I did. I don't remember if my mother was home or if anyone was home with me that day. We lived in a pretty safe neighborhood where everybody watched out for each other, so walking to the store wasn't unusual or going with a family friend didn't require permission as long as someone knew where you were. But this day was different. This day my brother's best friend raped me. At the age of 12 he stole my innocence and changed the course of my life forever. A guy who had essentially been a part of our family for many, many years. He slept and ate at our house. But yet, he had this ugly craving to rape a pencil thin, young girl who was helpless.

The day went like this: **Him** – "hey come walk with me to the store." We walked to the candy store all the time, and we always took a short cut. At the end of our street was an alley that led to a field. We walked through the field or "the cut", as we use to call it, every day to get to McDonald's, to school and to the candy store. The cut led to McDonald's parking lot and over to another street. We had to cross the street to get to the store or to school. And this day wasn't any different.

As we walked, I'm sure we made small talk because I was a very talkative child. I rambled a lot, as my grandmother used to say. But as we were walking down another side street, I remember "him" saying, I need to stop at this house and grab something. It was an abandoned house that also backed up to woods. I wasn't afraid because I was with someone that I trusted. He was grown and roughly 6'7". We went through the back door, which led into the kitchen. We walked through the dining room and into the living room. In the living room was an old couch. It looked like it had been left by the previous tenants or pulled off the curb. It was torn with stains all over it. I remember the house being very creepy. As we walked, the wooden floors creaked. He was standing close behind me, and I thought he was there to protect me. As the floors continued to make noise as if the entire house was "settling", I said to him, "I'm scared and I'm ready to go." He looked at me and didn't say a word. As I looked away from him, he grabbed me, twisted my arms behind my back, shoved me on that nasty sofa – face down and put his knee in my back. I couldn't scream. I couldn't scream because I was scared to death as hot tears rolled down my face. I remember as he was pulling my shorts down, my fear turned into anger and I started wiggling to try to get free. Because of his sheer size compared to mine, I couldn't move much. I couldn't believe what he was doing to me. Why me? What did I do to deserve this? He towered over me so I physically could not move. And after he got finished, he made me pull my shorts up, led me out the house and kindly walked me back home as if nothing ever happened. I had just been raped by my brother's best friend and everyone around me was clueless. Thoughts went through my head like: they won't believe me, so why say anything. And, what if I say something and he comes back to hurt me again?

When we got back to my house, I went to my room and just cried. I ran me some bath water and tried to scrub a layer of skin off of my body; trying to scrub away his scent and the memory of what happened. I cried and I scrubbed. I scrubbed some more and I cried. But no matter how much scrubbing I did, nothing could block out what had just happened. The thoughts kept replaying in my mind, over and over again "he raped me!" It was like a nightmare that turned into reality.

Later on that night I mustered up enough courage to tell my mother. I was scared to death. What if she didn't believe me? What if she thought it was my fault. My mother's opinion mattered to me. She was the strongest woman that I knew and I didn't want to hurt her or make her mad. She was a no-nonsense kind of woman who took pride in teaching her children (all 7 of us) right from wrong. She was there to protect us from all dangers.

I don't recall the look on her face as I told her what happened, but I do recall that nothing ever happened to him. Did she not believe me? Did she not know what to do? Our family, like every other black family growing up in the 60's and 70's had that one special rule "What goes on in this house, stays in this house." And as my mother was holding on to this mentality…I was slowly dying on the inside. At that moment, I made an unconscious decision to never share my feelings or emotions with anyone in my family ever again.

Maybe mom did what she knew how to do. Maybe she had never experienced what I was going through. Maybe she really didn't know how to protect her children like I thought she did…maybe, maybe, maybe. If she couldn't protect me…who could? If she didn't feel strong enough to fight for me…who would? What if it happened again, who would I tell? Why didn't she tell my sisters and brothers? Surely they would have comforted me. I was 12 years old for crying out loud. I didn't do anything to deserve this. And as I cried, this rape became my secret.

He had stopped coming around for a while; and I later learned that he had joined the army. I was relieved, even at a young age, to know that I didn't have to worry about him anymore.

As I got older, GOD began to deal with me. I always wanted to know where GOD was when I was getting attacked. Why my rapist chose me and why it happened. I didn't really know GOD, but I always saw my mother and oldest brother reading the bible in the living room and debating over the content of the scriptures. Did GOD not love me because HE allowed this to happen? Why didn't HE stop it? I never got the answers, but I still found a reason to praise HIM.

I was the first of many rapes by my attacker. And as the years went by, I learned that the attacks became more and more vicious. When I was in my late 30's I heard on the news that my attacker had been arrested for the abduction, rape and <u>murder</u> of two young girls…who were the same age that I was when he raped me. He had become dark and sinister. He had taken his rape game to a whole new level. Raping kids wasn't enough for him...it must have gotten boring – I don't know. But his exploration into abducting and killing little girls was pure evil. I don't remember how long the first trial lasted but he was sentenced to life in prison. While he was serving time for the one rape and murder, charges were brought up against him on the second rape and murder. This time he was sentenced to death.

This attack grossly reminds me of Tamar in 2nd Samuel 13. Tamar was a virgin and she was raped at the hands of her half-brother Amnon; and her father King David did nothing to punish him. It became apparent that King David was more focused on protecting the abuser than the victim. However, a few years later, Tamar's older brother Absalom ordered Amnon to be killed. Now, there's no gracious ending to this story. She didn't ride off with Prince Charming. And it doesn't mention if Tamar ever got married or had children. But one thing we do know, is that she survived. And if she survived, God's hand had to be on her life. God doesn't allow us to survive situations just for the sake of survival, but to show us that His grace is sufficient and we ought to run back like the 1 leper and give Him glory.

I ran back and gave God glory. Yes I got raped. Yes I was only 12. Yes he stole my virginity and innocence. But I thank GOD for protecting me and allowing me to be <u>first.</u> He didn't hurt me, as I can imagine he did those other two little girls. I could have been one of his last victims and you would not be reading this book...but GOD.

My rapist died in 2013 in prison. A slow and painful death of pancreatic cancer. The funny thing is; I had no emotion when I received the news. I didn't have the guts to even rejoice. If GOD forgave him (and I hope he asked for forgiveness before he died), who was I to hold on to the pain and allow a man who was dead to have control over my life. Additionally, I know my mother loved me unconditionally. So maybe – just maybe instead of letting the police and media in on what my attacker did to me, maybe she prayed for me and my mental state and that's why the attack never consumed my life. I don't know – and I may never know. But whatever the case; maybe GOD provided a way of escape, and therefore I choose to hold on to the fact that GOD is **#MyProtector.** Thank God I don't look like what I've been through.

Psalm 91:1-16, *but I want to focus on* **v1** *(He that dwelleth in the secret place of the most High shall abide under the shadow of the Almighty.)* GOD hid me and protected me. *And* **v8** *(Only with thine eyes shalt thou behold and see the reward of the wicked.)* HE restored me and allowed me to see the reward of my attacker. I didn't have to do anything but stand still and let GOD be GOD.

CHAPTER 2 – MY KEEPER

I just wanted to be loved and protected, so by the age of 14, I had started dating. He was an older guy (16) and the first time he told me that he loved me…he had me hook, line and sinker. He told me what I wanted to hear when I needed to hear it. He was my everything. He was my first love and he *seemed* to care about my wellbeing, so I clung to him. And as most first loves go – I simply adored him. I was so in love (yes, at 14) and no one could tell me anything. He romanced me and the more he did, the more I fell head over hills. He knew that I was vulnerable and wouldn't leave him no matter what. And the "no matter what" turned into him dating 2-3 girls at the same time and we all knew about each other. But I was the special one…so I thought. He was the first guy that I had sex with (other than the rape) and I knew he was the one for me. He didn't make me feel dirty, like the rape. He made me feel safe…unlike the rape. He protected me…unlike – you get the picture. In addition to the lying and cheating he also encouraged all types of bad behavior, like flicking school to stay home with him; and drinking Golden Champale. I was never a big drinker, so a couple of sips had me woozy. It was becoming apparent (to everyone except for me) that I was spending too much time with him.

As a way of escape from the mind battles and yearning to be loved, I enjoyed running track. However, since I had started dating, track had become an afterthought. And by the age of 15 I had gotten pregnant. I hid the pregnancy from my mother for 2-3 months until the morning sickness kicked in and I had to tell her. I thought she would be happy for me. I was having a baby by the love of my life. Yeah, forget the fact that I was only 15, I was fighting (and most of the fights I started) and arguing with his other girlfriends on a regular basis – but he still loved me. I didn't expect the reaction from my mother that I received. She hit the roof! She was yelling and cussing; cussing and fussing and a few days later, she had scheduled me a "doctor's" appointment to take care of the baby. That procedure was so invasive and mentally draining. I went in with a baby and left empty and my self-esteem plummeted to an all-time low. I wanted that baby so bad. Not to keep the man, but to have someone that I could love and who would love me.

Raped, Abortion, Lied to, Betrayed...what could possibly happen next? How could someone so young endure so much? I was borderline depressed as suicidal thoughts scattered through my mind. I had no one to talk to. No one that I trusted. At 15 I had a fleeting thought of not wanting to live and then I met Mr. Right.

Ohhhh, Mr. Right was so smooth and oh so wrong. He had come from a single-parent home too, but somewhere along the way he learned the right things to say to woo me away from Mr. Wrong. He went to all lengths to impress me including battling in an actual fist fight with my ex. So now the tables were turned. Where I was fighting other girls, now boys were fighting for me. And any man that would fight for me had to be the one. And the winner took all...me!

Mr. Right could do no wrong. He too said the right words at the right time. He even went a step further and won the love and affection of my family...he had to be the one. He showered me with gifts, loved me, fought for me and I knew we would be together forever. By the age of 16 I delivered our first child. I had vowed that I would not endure another abortion, and since I was still a minor – my mother still had the final say. So I did what any 16 year old would do, who was determined to have a baby, I hid my pregnancy until I was 6 months. Throughout my entire pregnancy I only gained 24 pounds. And on July 19, 1984 I delivered a beautiful bouncing baby boy. He was just as I had expected…perfect. My first true love. The love of my life. I wanted to give him the world. By the age of 18, Mr. Right was living with me at my mother's house and I was pregnant with my second child. By the age of 19, I was pregnant with our third child and my mother had finally had enough and put us out. I see where the saying "we don't die, we multiply" comes from because we were making babies like rabbits. Mr. Right was selling weed, not out of my mother's house, but selling it nonetheless to "provide for his children." We moved in together in the projects and we were happy. I was grown, living on my own and reality kicked in. I had 3 kids and a man but did not know how to cook or wash clothes. I played house for so long that when reality kicked in, it was too much. My sister came over to cook for me a couple of days per week, and then she decided to move to Boston. So now, who was going to feed us? I was ready to go back home to momma's house, but I had to prove to her that I could do this on my own.

Because I had so many babies, didn't have a job and was on welfare, we lived in the projects. I had some pretty cool neighbors. They were always home during the day and went to work at night. I didn't quite understand what their jobs were…until much later. However, I always noticed that they had different men going in and out of their apartment. At first I thought they were running a call-girl service; why else would so many people be going in and out so frequently. See, I was really sheltered; naïve even. I lived and grew up on the same street until I moved out, and my mom really didn't allow us to venture too far from home. One day when Mr. Right was out cheating; I assumed he was because he had been gone for several days; I asked my neighbor what was going on. I had lived there for a while now and we had gotten cool. Cool enough to where they felt comfortable enough to introduce me to the CRIPS. At the time, I had only heard horror stories about the CRIPS from California, gang banging with the Bloods (another gang in California), mean dudes who killed people; but these guys seemed different. Yea they "cripped walked" all the time and talked slang language that only they knew, but they were friendly. They made snide comments about people who wore red, but they were in a completely different state, where no one really understood the rivalry between the two gangs.

After hanging around them for a few weeks, I remember one of the guys asking me if I wanted to make some extra money. I was living in the projects. Baby daddy wasn't really around to help take care of the kids...so instead of curiosity killing the cat – I wanted to know more. I asked how and it was simply explained, all you have to do is sell some "work." **Me:** What's work? **Him:** Crack. **Me:** So, all I have to do is sell crack out of my home and you'll provide the product? That's it? **Him:** Yep, that's it and I'll show you how it's done. About a week later, they came over with some powder and cooked it up in my kitchen. I was so amazed how it transformed from a powder to a solid form. And of course I wanted to learn how to cook. In a couple of days I had made about a $1,000. I thought I was living the dream. Now that I'm wiser, I know that $1,000 is just a rounding error, but back then (1987) and living in the projects with three kids, I was desperate and could use all the cash I could get.

I had been selling work for about a month before I let baby daddy in on what was going on. Baby daddy aka Mr. Right...turned Mr. Wrong, was immediately excited and came back home to the land of milk and honey...were money was flowing freely. He had always been a hustler, so making a quick come up was right up his alley. I introduced him to the crew and it took our game to a whole new level. We were selling dope – balling out of control and making money hand over fist, all while still living in government housing. The crew from Cali started with 3 dudes and it turned into about 6 from their hood. Before we knew it we had an entire organization set up with operations in Akron, Canton, Brimfield, Cleveland and Youngstown. They had become like family I always wanted.

I was now pregnant with our 4th child. We were living the American dream of getting rich and destroying lives and we were blind to it all. We had invited these guys into our homes and we loved and trusted them. If someone didn't pay, all I had to do was make one phone call and the situation was handled. If someone got smart, all I had to do was tell one of my "brothers" and it was taken care of. There was so much dysfunction in my life, that even when the truth was spoken I didn't believe it. There were shoot outs, parties for days, people getting beat up because we were taking their business, money being made in five different cities and we thought we were untouchable. Mr. Right had gotten head strong and he was openly cheating. He was always a boastful man, so flaunting his money and what he had was normal.

I had a few people give me some warnings

about our activities, but I didn't heed any of them. I knew that we were being investigated, but I also thought our team ran the world. I was so blind and naïve to reality. I was literally living in a nightmare.

Back in the day we use to change our phone numbers every month to try to trip up the police from putting a trace on our phones. One day I changed my number and had not given it to anyone (not even baby daddy) but I received a phone call from someone asking for one of the dudes. I was so dumb founded as to how anyone had gotten my number. I knew then that the law was starting to catch up to us. I mentioned it to Mr. Right and we had decided to get out the game. We had enough money saved up to where we would be good for a few years, if we cut back on our spending and partying. We were going to "re-up" one more time and go out with a bang.

That night, I stayed home with the kids and he left to buy two kilos...the last hoorah!

By the age of 21, I was 8 1/2 months pregnant with our 4th child and on my way to the federal penitentiary for 10 years...charged with conspiracy to distribute a controlled substance and possession of a firearm. The bust happened so quickly. When they kicked in my door I was asleep with my daughter nestled under my arm, my two boys were in their bedroom asleep and my babysitter was in another room asleep. Mr. Right was still gone from the previous night of picking up the two kilos and I was scared to death. All I heard was a loud noise, (which I later found out they used a batter-ram to bust down my front and back door) and about 8 US SWAT team members ran up my stairs. They had no idea what they were going to encounter when they entered my apartment and they weren't taking any chances. They were yelling, "get on the floor". At 8 1/2 months pregnant it was difficult to move, let alone get on the floor. They asked me about weapons in the house, and I just so happened to have a 9mm under my bed. Once they secured the firearm and saw that I wasn't a threat, they calmed down just a little. They continued to ask a million and one questions and I was so overwhelmed. They let the baby sitter leave and let me call my mother so she could come and get my kids. My first thought was, if I could just get in contact with one of my new "brother's" or Mr. Right all would be well. However, to my surprise, when I got outside of my apartment, 8 ½ months pregnant and handcuffed, the scene was out of a movie. SWAT team was everywhere. They had the entire complex blocked off with school buses, paddy wagons and unmarked police cars. Little did I know – until I got to the federal building, the

Feds had organized a strategic and calculated bust to ensure that we were all apprehended at the same time – with the exception of Mr. Right because they didn't know his whereabouts. There were 66 of us...all handcuffed, sitting and standing in a large room in the federal building. About 3 hours after we were detained, I heard the feds celebrating and applauding. They had finally caught up with Mr. Right and all chances of getting out of there were slim to none. We had no one to call. There was no way out. I had never received a traffic ticket...so I thought that I would be out in a matter of hours. I knew nothing about the law, heck I didn't even think what I was doing was wrong...I was just providing for my family. I was so naïve, and I quickly learned differently.

I was arrested June 1, 1989 at 6am. They had given me a $100,000 bond and 10% of it had to be paid to get out. All the money that we had,

had been confiscated, so I was broke. I was devastated to say the least. The first of many thoughts was "I cannot deliver my baby in jail." And "what's going to happen to my other kids at home?" "Who's going to raise them?" Surely they are not going to send me to jail. This is not how it was supposed to end.

My father came to my rescue. He paid my bond and I was released after sitting in a jail cell for three days. I was mad, stressed out, broke and on the verge of being evicted and having premature labor pains. About a month and a half after my release, Mr. Right was still in jail and my contractions were coming frequently, so two of my girlfriends came to stay the night with me. My 4th baby, a beautiful little boy, was born on July 19, 1989 – exactly five years from the date of my first son.

When my baby was one month old, the

courts revoked my bound for threatening a witness. Someone that I had taken care of, provided for and trusted had secretly snitched on me and my family. She was one of the key witnesses in my case. I really didn't think that would I said to her was wrong. Honestly, I was just talking junk to the girl and didn't have it in my heart to kill her if I wanted to – but the prosecutor took it seriously. I went to court and was immediately put back in jail where I stayed for five months until they sentenced me to 10 years in the federal penitentiary. I guess since I was affiliated with the CRIPS, they didn't know what I was capable of or if I had contact with other members and the justice system were not taking any chances. They locked me up, took the key and through it way.

In spite of my circumstances, I Praise God that He was **#MyKeeper**. The men used me, society through me way…But God Kept me. He kept me through the betrayals, through the heartache and even when I was out of control. His hand of Grace and Mercy was steadfast. And for that, I thank God that I don't look like what I went through.

CHAPTER 3 – MY SAVIOR

Talking about a hard blow. Four children, 21 years old and facing 10 years. I was bitter. For the first year, I didn't cry...I was just mad. Mad at the world for a situation that I had created. Mad because I didn't have control. Within the first two years I had filed several appeals and they were all denied; and now I was set on doing my time...I had no other choice.

I was in a federal prison, so my time wasn't that bad. The best thing about where they sent me was that it was co-ed. The women and men did everything together...and I do mean everything; except sleep in the same units. Everyone was shacked up with a man and covering up for the next couple to do what they had to do, even the prison guards. I honestly believe that even though I was locked up, away from my family and children – my family had the short end of the deal. I had the luxury of having a man, tennis courts, movie theatres, skating, and basketball, a hair salon, we were able to wear our clothes and more...I just didn't have my freedom and my children.

About a year of the facility being co-ed, all of the men were shipped out because too many women were getting pregnant and the warden could not tell if the female inmates were pregnant by the guards or by the male inmates. After baby number 4, I had my tubes clipped, tied and burned, so I was safe. I had been dating Mr. Columbia for 9 months. We even had a mock/fake wedding in jail. And the best part was that he didn't speak that much English and he didn't need to, as long as we both understood the universal language of sex.

After the men were shipped out, more

women were shipped in and chaos ensued. There were fights every day. Hormones were raging out of control, with over 2,000 women living on one campus there were fights every day. More and more butch women were shipped in and since the women no longer had the luxury of a real man – other than the guards, the butch women filled that gap. Those who were not hooked up with a butch, were secretly dating the male guards and sometimes both.

Most of the guards were male, married and hungry for something different. Their appetite to venture outside of their marriages broke up a lot of happy homes. Most of the guards were caught because their prison "girlfriend" either got pregnant or dumped. And since the male inmates had been shipped out to all male facilities, the warden knew that it had to be one of his guards. When a girl got dumped, she would set-up the guard to be busted bringing in contraband. The prison openly walked these guards out handcuffed, so you knew immediately when someone had gotten busted. The benefits of dating a guard; everything that wasn't on the prisons approved list, the guards brought in like, perfume, weave, hair dye, money and gum. All the things that make a girl feel like a girl – all at the expense of the guards freedom, their job and their marriage. Heck, we had nothing to lose, we were already locked up.

I had run with some rough cats on the streets, so doing time with these chicks was not a problem. I came in with a bad attitude, smart mouth, and chip on my shoulder and I was able to hold my own. While doing time, I only got into two fights and both were over a man (best believe that I don't do that anymore), and I won them both. The rule was that when we fought we watched each other's backs when we were banging. Win or lose we didn't want anyone going to hole. We preferred that the loser walk around the grounds so everyone could see the effects of the beat down. That was justice enough for you running your mouth. We only went to the hole if the person who lost snitched, if we got busted by a guard, or if the chick was dating a guard and <u>he</u> got mad. I was lucky to only be sent to the hole once for beating up a chick that was dating a guard. It's safe to say that he wasn't too happy. It was true isolation and I believe this is when God started tugging at my heart.

I only stayed in the hole for a week but it was long enough for me to know I had had enough of life as it was. I was now going to church often. I had gotten baptized and was trying to live somewhat right. It wasn't easy and most days I failed miserably. I was still cussing people out

EVERY day. Doing everything I wasn't supposed to do, but I knew that I wanted to be and do better. I was just stuck in this vicious cycle called life...prison life. A life that I had created by one bad decision after another. I was living like I wanted to live with minimal to no consideration for the consequences. The temptations to continue to do wrong were real, but my heart was telling me differently. I knew I wanted to change, but didn't know how. My older brother was an ordained pastor and I found myself calling him periodically to ask him questions about the bible. None of the things really stuck, but God was beginning to draw me. I didn't understand it then, but He was drawing me.

After being in prison for about 4 years, I had to have surgery to have my tonsils removed. I remember the doctor asking me if I was allergic to any medications and I told him yes. He asked,

"What happens when you take it?" and I told him that I didn't know – my mother just always told me never to take it. The doctor figured that the side effects would be minimal so he decided to give me a shot and walked out of the room. All I remember is that within 5 minutes I became light headed, dizzy and extremely hot. I was in the room all alone and I knew immediately that something was wrong. I wasn't going to lie in that bed and die. I was too dizzy to walk and my vision was blurred, so I got off the bed and started crawling. That hospital floor felt like heaven. It was ice cold and all I wanted to do was hug it; but I knew I had to get someone's attention. All I remember was crawling and I woke up hours later with tubes running everywhere. The devil was trying to take me out and he used this doctor who didn't have enough sense to stick around and see how the drugs would have an effect on me.

But why? I wasn't a threat…at least back then I wasn't. The thing is (and I learned this from my Pastor) the devil fights us based on where GOD is taking us, not where we currently are or what our current situation makes us believe we are. So because the devil knew that I was fearfully and wonderfully made…in GOD's image; and that one day I would be a force to be reckoned with, he was trying to take me out the game early. I love the saying "GOD looks after the elderly, babies and fools." And since I wasn't old or a baby, I guess that put me in the fool category…I was just glad HE dispatched HIS angels to my side, even when I didn't know I needed them.

I had now been in federal prison for 7 years and in 3 different facilities. I spent 5 years in Lexington, KY and then moved to California's maximum security facility and was there for 1 year. While there I got into another fight and this time I got beat. In Kentucky, chicks fought over their man/woman. In Cali these chicks fought just to fight and man those Cali chicks were no joke. I thought I could fight until I ran up against a real rough neck. When they were on the streets, these girls fought as a means of survival. This chick hit me so hard in my eye that all I could see were black spots for about a week. It was either put up or shut up and that day I got shut up and down.

It had been over 1 year since I saw my children and my family and I was sick. Sick of doing time and sick of being so far away from home. Not long after the fight I put in for a transfer to get closer to home and was granted approval to move to a camp in North Carolina. The camp was sweet...there were 4 guards to cover the grounds, doors never locked, but there was absolutely nothing...and I do mean nothing to do there but work.

While in NC, my grandmother had fallen ill and passed away. I was informed that in order for me to go home for the funeral, I would be required to pay for two US Marshalls to travel with me and pay for their hotel, food and travel accommodations. I was devastated that I couldn't go home and pay my final respects to my grandmother. I couldn't catch a break.

In the mist of my misery, I called my father just to talk, mostly about nothing to take my mind off of prison life. During our small talk he told me he had seen on the news that a new law had passed regarding gun charges. If a gun had not been used in the commission of a crime, a person could not be charged. I had mixed emotions about the news because I had already exhausted all of my appeals; and the attorney that I was originally using was court appointed and he had sold me out. He never fought for my rights – and I had no idea what to do. After toying with this new information for about a week, I wrote a letter to my sentencing judge and explained my case and to my surprise he assigned me a new attorney. This attorney was night and day compared to my trial attorney. This guy explained the new law to me, told me what my probably of winning my appeal was and within 4 months I had a new court date. Everything he told me was true. I went to court, hand cuffed and shackled, I won my appeal, and was released immediately...right there in the court room. I remember the look on my mom and children's faces when the judge told them that I was free to go. It took about two hours for them to release me and when they did, my family was waiting outside.

This entire ordeal was eye-opening. I was no better than the thief who hung on the cross next to Jesus (Luke 23:32-43). I suffered justly because of my sins and Jesus was right there with me. The things that I did put me in a situation that only God could save me from. But in order for Him to free me – I first had to confess my sins and that He was Lord and savior.

Even though I did 7 years in prison, GOD never left me nor forsook me. I found a reason to praise Him and thank Him for sending me to prison for the simple fact that while serving time, I was re-introduced to Him and I got saved and baptized. Before prison, GOD was the last thing on my mind. If I hadn't gone, I probably would not have been introduced to GOD…and I was introduced to HIM on a whole new level. People always make comments and jokes about criminals finding GOD when they go to jail…and I was one of them and thank Him for allowing our paths to cross. There's a song that says "GOD thought I was to die for…so I could be free", and I'm so glad that

HE sacrificed HIS life for me. I wasn't worthy...but HE saved me. I was okay living in my mess – but HE saw fit to call me and set me free (naturally and spiritually). Jesus saved my life, by snatching me off the streets. HE saved my life when the doctor's tried to kill me. HE saved my life when I accepted salvation. Yes indeed - I found a reason to praise HIM. **#MySavior**. Thank God I don't look like what I've been through.

2 Samuel 22:3 *"The LORD is my rock and my fortress and my deliverer; My God, my rock, in whom I take refuge, My shield and the horn of my salvation, my stronghold and my refuge; My savior, You save me from violence."*

CHAPTER 4 – MY PROVIDER

When I came home in 1996, I still had some of my mannish ways. GOD had saved me but I had not been delivered from a lot of things. I wanted to recoup some of my lost time. I had been away from my kids for 7 years. I was with them during the day and at every club in the city at night. I was trying to make up for lost time. I had been home 4 months and since baby daddy was still in jail, I literally partied all 4 months and it was starting to get old. More importantly, it was time to deal with reality and start looking for a job. When I was selling dope, I got addicted to the fast money.

My children and I had everything we wanted and needed...before jail; and now that I was home, things were different. I was broke. I went from having an unlimited amount of funds to making $6.50 an hour to take care of 4 kids.

This was not how I had imagined my life would be.

I contemplated going back to that life of luxury...but had no clue where to start, who to trust and how to do it without going back to jail. I remember a "friend" giving me some work to sell to help me get on my feet. I held on to it for about a week and flushed it down the toilet. At that point I made a decision that that wasn't my life anymore and jail was no longer an option. All of my "connections" from 7 years ago, were either still in jail or had moved out of the city and I had no way of contacting them. I didn't trust anyone; after all, some of the ones I trusted were the ones who testified against me. The life that I had once grown so accustomed to was now a thing of the past; and the struggle was real.

While in jail I worked in the warden's office which was a part of Unicore (a manufacturing company inside the prison that employed inmates and it paid slave wages, like $2.50 an hour. I learned a lot of clerical skills, so it was easy finding a temporary job. The hard part was finding a full time job that paid well enough with just a high school diploma. I worked my temporary job for about 13 months until I was hired in full time making $7.25 an hour. With the increase in my salary, I no longer qualified for food stamps, which was a saving grace when trying to feed 4 children. The only good thing was that my mother moved to Boston and allowed me and the kids to live in her house rent free. So the money that I saved on rent went to buy food. I worked an entry level job for several years and worked overtime every chance I got to make ends meet.

I realized that if I was going to be a role model for my kids in spite of my past, I needed to make some changes; so in June 1998 I enrolled in college. From my experience with the courts, I knew that I wanted to be a court reporter. They made good money and aside from the judge, they ran the courtroom. If they couldn't understand the discussions enough to document the trials, the court reporter would stop the proceedings and have each party repeat what was said. They had power and I wanted some of it. I went to school for three years and I was at the top of my class. I was typing 200+ words per minute. Over the past two years my focus was to learn legal and medical terminology because those were the cases that made the most money. I was good. I had ordered a new machine that translated the "shorthand" words to "real" words and was focused on graduation. I excelled through the first 2 years and had about 6-8 months left of school. I was excited about life.

It was a cool September night in 2001, exactly four days after the twin towers had been destroyed and the entire country was in turmoil and mourning. I had finally saved up enough money to move out of my mom's house and me and the kids moved into our own place. We had only been in our home for a little over a month. Two of my children were at their school's homecoming dance that night and after homecoming they went to eat at what use to be one of their favorite, but cheap restaurants. They got home around 11pm or so that night and I believe I was already in the bed sleeping.

    I remember receiving a call around 6am the next morning from my mom. She had gotten a call around midnight the night before that completely changed her world. A call that changed the dynamics of our family. I still remember her shaky voice when she told me that my little brother had been killed…hit by a car as he was running across a street. He was 31 years old, my baby brother, my twin (some would say); same mother and father. Oh I loved him, but I was upset with him when he died and the guilt of never seeing him again was horrible. I had a lot of "what if" mind battles that I didn't know how to deal with. I cried for hours before I woke my kids up to tell them the news. The ironic thing was, the night before, as the kids were coming home from dinner; they saw the aftermath of the accident. The police were there and had covered my brother's body up so passerby's could not see him. My children saw "a" body covered up with a white sheet, lying in the middle of the road and they had no idea it was their uncle. We were all devastated to say the least.

My mother had just lost her baby boy, my little brother. How do you help your grieving mother? At the time, I had no idea. I was dealing with my own guilt and emotions, while my mother had to deal with the loss of her child emotionally on her own. She had other people around who loved and missed my brother, but I know firsthand that no one can ease the pain of losing a child but God. And to be honest, at the time none of our lives represented God. We didn't read our bibles, we went to church periodically, but we didn't have a real relationship with God. So we all struggled emotionally. We weren't fit to help one another in this area because we didn't have the tools. The tools of prayer and intercession. But maybe God was showing Himself to her. Maybe He had given her peace that surpassed all understanding. I've learned that when we fall short, which we all have and will again, God always comes through to show Himself true. God has a way of tending to our broken hearts even when we fail to acknowledge Him, live for Him and fall short. He has a way of stepping in and making things better simply because He is God and God alone.

A few months had passed and life for me went back to normal, but not for my mother. I missed my little brother, but I poured my waking hours into my kids, work and school. I remember my son, Thomas, told me that he had a dream about my brother. They were outside walking and he stepped off of the curb and was almost hit by a car, but my brother grabbed him by the collar and snatched him back. He said the dream was so real that he woke up in a sweat. I tried to normalize the vision, but how can you when you're not really connected spiritually? God wasn't speaking to me. God didn't give me a revelation. My interpretation of the dream was purely natural, and I missed the mark.

We were preparing for the Christmas holiday. It was a little different without my brother, but I was living in my own house now and I had to try to make the best out of this holiday for my children. My first grandchild was born a month prior and I was just ecstatic. My kids still spent a lot of time at my mother's house…almost every weekend and this particular weekend was no different. It was mid-December and my mother and I were attending a Christmas party at my aunt's house. It was cold outside, but I don't recall there being much snow out. About 6pm that night, my son Thomas rode his bike to the gas station to get some candy. He had the cross-walk and proceeded across the street. About mid-way across he was hit by a drunk driver. The accident completely broke his right leg from his hip to his ankle and he had a concussion.

What was going on? Why was all of this hell breaking loose in our family…in our lives? My family hadn't quite recovered from the loss of my brother just 3 months prior and now this.

Since he had gotten hit over the weekend, he had to remain in a body traction and heavily sedated for the pain until Monday when the surgeons returned. The first surgery went well and he remained in the hospital for a few days. He was completely bed-ridden for 4 months. He was 16 years old, 5'7" and I remember we had to carry him to the bathroom, give him sponge baths and wait on him hand and foot. He was not allowed to leave his bed…unless we carried him. This meant I had to take a full family leave from my job. A leave that meant "no work – no pay". I was off of work for 3 full months, I had to drop out of school, and had little to no adult interaction. My now 17 year old son and the 4 walls were beginning to close in on me. I had to go back to work…even if it was part time. I was depressed, losing weight and desperately needed some adult interaction because I was beginning to lose my mind. By mid-March – my son was well enough to come downstairs on his own for the first time in 3 months. He had a tutor that came over every morning and helped him with his school work, and in the afternoon I went to work. By April, I was back at work full time.

PRAISE BREAK: The funny thing is, during these 4 months…I had absolutely no income coming in and I never missed a house payment, we had plenty of food to eat and no utility was ever disconnected. How? Luke 12:24 reminds us that if God can cover and feed the birds of the air, how much more valuable are we. GOD made a way. Just like He sent the ravens to feed Elijah in 1 Kings 17:6; He unctioned my co-workers to take a financial collection for me because He knew my situation was serious. Not only that, they prepared meals for me and the kids 3 times a week and brought it to our home every week that I was off work. GOD was showing me then that HE was my provider no matter my situation. I found a reason to praise HIM because HE's Jehovah Jireh. Yes, I was barely making ends meet with $10.50 an hour. Yes, I was barely getting by. Yes, my brother was killed and yes, my son was hit by a car but God showed Himself to be my Prince of Peace and my son's protector. He took a life, but He spared a life. Our lives were in turmoil but He covered us, shielded us from dangers seen and unseen and made a way out of no way. I had absolutely no income coming in for 4 months but through it all GOD was building my trust and faith in HIM. I found a reason to praise HIM. **#MyProvider.** **#MySon'sProtector** **#MyFamily'sPrinceofPeace**. Thank God I don't look like what I've been through.

Philippians *4:19 "And my God will supply every need of yours according to his riches in glory in Christ Jesus." God provided all of my needs (financial, mental and spiritual) – even when I didn't have enough common sense to understand that it was working together for the good of those who loved HIM.*

CHAPTER 5 – MY WAYMAKER

Somewhere between getting sentenced to 10 years in prison, being baptized, to almost dying in jail, I realized my self-worth and made a decision to never date another Mr. Wrong. I didn't care what his potential was. If he showed the slightest sign of a cheater...I was out. If he talked a lot of game, with no results...I was out. If he asked to borrow money...I was out. If he sold drugs...I was out. If he never paid for dinner...I was out. If he didn't take care of his kids...I was out. If he didn't respect his momma or daddy, I was out. I had 4 kids who totally depended on me so I had to be on top of my game. I wasn't looking for a man to take care of me; I did that on my own. But he had to, at a minimum, complement what I already had. Before jail, my definition of a good man was if he sexed me good, I was down forever. If he told me he loved me, I would never leave his side. If he told me I was the only one even if I had proof that I wasn't, I was going to be his ride or die chick forever. After jail, he had a 6 month waiting period before he was considered my man and he had to prove all of the above and more. I turned guys off instantly because they just couldn't run game anymore. By the age of 21, the first two dudes taught me lessons of a lifetime. They taught me that I didn't need a man who didn't add value to my life. I didn't need a man who wanted to control me mentally or physically. I didn't need a man who just made me feel good. I didn't need a man to tell me what to do. I didn't need a man that I would have to take care of. I didn't need a man that was a liar. I had all of that in the past and I ended up used, broken, misused and in jail. The only good things out of this were my four children. **For my LADIES**: It's okay to have standards, but they should be realistic standards.

If not, there's a possibility that you will end up again with the same thing you just got finished running from.

It took about two full years for my son to fully recover, to the point where he no longer had to attend physical therapy and no longer required the use of a wheelchair or walking on a cane or crutches. It was a long, painful journey with multiple surgeries – but he made it through and came out even stronger. We had found a little normalcy in our lives. I had received a couple promotions within the past two years and even though I was still struggling to make ends meet, we were getting by. I was a very private and prideful person. A lot of people in the family thought that I had it going on – when I barely had two nickels to rub together. The funny thing was, even though I was barely making over minimum wage, paying full rent, taking care of four children, with no assistance from the government, I never received an eviction notice and utilities never got cut off. GOD made my struggle look easy and therefore no one ever offered a helping hand, but always had a hand out for help. There was a spirit of determination on me and I was set on making things right for my kids. They had already been through so much with both parents in jail, that at this point, failure and going back to jail were no longer an option.

I had been dating the *real* Mr. Right a.k.a. Mr. Wonderful for about 5 years and we had finally made the decision to move in together. I wasn't saved for real and he didn't even know what being saved meant, but he was a good man. He worked, opened the car door for me, paid for all our dinners and movies and he showed a little interest in my children. He met most of my requirements and that was all I needed. I knew that this man right here was no counterfeit. We dated for about seven months before he met my children and about one year before I met his. I believe my oldest son and my step-daughter met in high school before we formally introduced them. I didn't have time to entertain no mess, dope boys were a thing of the past and not working, going to school or at least trying to get on the right path was a straight turn off. We both wanted and needed to be sure that we were the "one."

But man, let me tell you, Mr. Wonderful got a rude awakening when he moved in with "us." The boys were cool, even though they had to go through a huge adjustment of knocking on my bedroom door before walking in. But that daughter of mine...whew – let's just leave it right here. She was a handful, a mouthful and even a few slaps and chokes later, didn't change her much. If you can, imagine an extreme, hormone raging, teenage girl, who hated everyone – this was her. She woke up mad and went to bed mad. When she walked, she stomped up the stairs, slammed the door, stomped back down the stairs and slammed another door. If you asked her a question she either got smart or didn't answer at all. One day when she was mad, she even had the nerve to try to elbow Mr. Wonderful back down the stairs. He was livid…and I, well, let's just say that if the same children service protection laws for whooping kids were in place then as they are now, I probably would have lost my kids. This child had lost her mind. She was a spoiled rotten, disrespectful brat and I had had enough. I know without a shadow of a doubt that God was working on me then because she should have been dead if it weren't for His hand on my life. This went on for about 2 years, and then one day she woke up and she was a normal, sweet teenage girl. It was like a thief had come in the middle of the night and stole what they thought was our most precious gem, but in all actuality took the cubic zirconia a.k.a. her bad attitude.

Mr. Wonderful moved in with me, three of my children, my nephew, my sister-in-law and her two kids and somewhere down the road, my grandson's mom moved in and my daughter's then boyfriend. It was like growing up at my mom's house all over again. As you can see, my problem was not helping people, but turning them away. If they needed a place to live, my door was open. If they were hungry, I fed them. If they needed money, I gave to them. I believe my mother planted the seed of giving from the heart and God came along and watered it. I wanted to save everybody.

Every time I came home there was a new

neighborhood kid there. I think my kids wanted to save everyone too. Some of the kids were there so frequent that they had chores too. There were special ones who stole my heart and then there were some fly by night kids who came by once or twice. My house was a revolving door. I loved that God had provided for us enough to give back to those less fortunate. However, this was starting to wear on Mr. Wonderful. He was the youngest of six and didn't grow up with kids or noise for that matter in the house. So "adjusting" to this new environment was an understatement. He was use to quiet – and it was far from quiet in our house. He was use to privacy – and with 3-4 adults and 7-10 kids at most times, there was no privacy. And even though I was used to being in chaotic environments, this was a huge sacrifice for him. We hardly had any alone time, and it was starting to wear on our relationship. He definitely made all of the sacrifices in the relationship; because I was too focused on me and my children. I was on a mission to succeed and I hadn't quite figured out what success meant; but I was more than sure I knew what it wasn't.

It took us a few years to adjust to living together. So as I struggled to not only take care of my family, I now had the ultimate task of taking care of others. And as I look back on time, I know that GOD made a way out of no way. I wasn't living right in the sight of GOD nor was I raising my kids' right in the sight of GOD, but I loved His children...all of them. They didn't have to be "blood family" to receive help. I watched my mother for many years, sacrificing her time, money and energy to help others and she never complained about receiving anything in return and unbeknownst to me, I unconsciously found myself doing the same. So where others would have given up on these families and kids – I gave all I had. It was hard carrying the responsibility of these families, but God made a way. I had to make sure they had a roof over their heads, food to eat, utilities stayed on and sometimes I had to buy shoes and clothes. I didn't have it to give, but God made a way. Some days I wanted to run away and never return; but I couldn't afford to, and God made a way and gave me peace within my home. I had many of days and nights where it was a struggle to keep going, but I found a reason to praise God because HE proved over and over again to be my **#WayMaker.** Never give up when it gets hard; and know that God always has your back. I thank God I don't look like what I've been through.

CHAPTER 6 – MY DELIVERER

Let's fast forward to 2004. My home life was starting to wear on me. I had been on my job for 8 years now and they were starting to act crazy too. In addition, my kids were getting buck wild. I couldn't quite pin point why hell was starting to break lose on all ends of my life again, but it was becoming unbearable. I knew that I needed to get away, so I had planned to take the kids to Disney World in Orlando. I had it all planned out that in February 2005, a week before my son Thomas' birthday, we would go.

The night sweats; which were periodically, were coming regularly to the point where I was waking up every night to change my clothes because they were soaked with sweat. The sweat covered my body like dew covers the grass on a fresh spring morning. I would literally have to dry off with a towel before putting on new pajamas. And during the day, it was anxiety attacks. So bad to where I could barely catch my breath when one hit me. I didn't understand what was going on, other than the fact that I was overwhelmed. I was working full time, going to school full time, taking care of my kids and grandkids full time, playing house with Mr. Wonderful full time...but I had no time for me. We were scheduled to leave for vacation on February 19, 2005 a few days before my son Thomas' birthday. But as luck would have it on February 17th at 9am in the morning I was sitting at my desk at work and my vision became blurred. Then I experienced a burning sensation in my left arm. It felt like someone had just lit my arm and chest on fire. I immediately knew that something was wrong so I sent my sister and email at work. She called me and I told her that I thought I was having a heart attack. I remember calling the receptionist at my job and told her that I needed some pure aspirin. After hanging up with the receptionist, I tried to go to the restroom, but I could barely see, my chest and arm still felt like they were on fire and I had no strength in my legs. Someone called the paramedics and I was rushed to the hospital where I remained in ICU for a 7 days.

I was 38 years old. I had been raped, had an abortion, gave birth to four children, spent seven years in a federal penitentiary, almost died in prison, lost everything and had to start over when I got out, (I didn't have two wooden nickels to rub together) and I just had a heart attack. Why was the devil beating on my door trying to kill me? He had sent a legion of devils out to attack me since the time I was a kid. What was he trying to stop? What was so valuable or important on my life that he needed to kill me...and immediately? Why was

I the target of these assassinations? He had been trying to kill me since I was a kid. What did he know about me that I didn't know about myself? These were all intentional attacks, strategically planned to either take me out or strengthen me. All I wanted was to live a normal life like everybody else; however, in return I found myself constantly fighting battles. Mind battles, trying not to lose my kids to the streets, trying to save other people's kids, and trying to strengthen my relationship with Mr. Wonderful. But instead I was now fighting for my life. I couldn't die...I had so much stuff that I still needed to do.

I was in the middle of exams that week in school, we were supposed to be leaving for vacation in two days, I still needed to get my hair "did", wash clothes, pack, and pick up the rental and so on. The devil was busy, but he didn't realize that I had my own agenda and I wasn't going out that easy. I was probably the worst patient that ICU staff had ever come across at that point; and I was too naïve to know that it was only by God's grace and mercy that I was still alive. As the doctors gave strict orders for me to lie flat on my back for 5 straight days as they ran tests, I refused. I called my mother and had her bring me food that wasn't allowed. I called Mr. Wonderful and told him to bring me my laptop so I could finish my finals. I called the hotel and told them that we would be two days late checking in and they needed to move our reservation out. I called my family and had visitors every hour. Everything that a heart attack patient shouldn't do – I did. Once again, as we know the saying "God takes care of the elderly, babies and fools"...and I'm sure I qualified under the fools headline again.

When I was released from the hospital I was given strict instructions not to travel. The doctors had performed an arterial catheterization in my groin and they were afraid that my artery would rupture. Being the great patient that I was, I insistently refused their orders and told them so. So they altered their instructions to say "if you travel, stop every 4-5 hours to stretch your legs to keep the blood flowing." Okay – well now I can live with those orders. I have to honestly say – that drive was theeeeeee, longest drive of my life. It took us 24 hours to get to Orlando because of all of the stops. Let me tell you, I can't thank God enough for watching over me and my family. I had to get there, I wanted to get there and at all costs, I got there.

My kids acted a complete fool. They say the fruit does not fall far from the tree and baby listen, I wanted to leave them all in Orlando. They argued, fought and argued some more. My youngest son even had the nerve to get out the car and start walking down a deserted street like he was back at home. Boy really? Wait until an alligator jumps out the swamp, let's see how far you get then. If I could have had a slap fest to knock some sense into them I would have. But I was afraid of going to back to jail, and this time facing the penalties in another state. I told Mr. Wonderful to drop them off at the nearest greyhound station but of course he refused. I was determined not to have another heart attack because they wanted to act a fool.

Mr. Wonderful and I had had enough for one day. It was about 8pm and we left the kids in the hotel and went out for a drive. We ended up at the beach and decided to go for a stroll along the shore. I just wanted some peace. It was March 5th and as we approached the beach, there was a horse drawn carriage sitting idle. The beach was vacant and the night was perfect. We decided to go for a ride on the horse drawn carriage and to my surprise my honey-boo proposed. Picture this; riding along the beach, stars gleaning on the water as the waves lightly slapped the shore. There was silence except for the horse's hooves echoing in the night. My head is resting on his arm that was wrapped around my shoulders, and I was hardly paying attention to anything because I was taking in the beauty of that night. He pulls out a piece of paper he had in his pocket and begins talking. He wrote a song that expressed his never-ending love, but because he was not a singer he decided to recite the words to me and then he asked the magic question..."will you marry me." I couldn't stop crying. I had just had a day from hell with my kids and after experiencing everything he had to go through with my family over the past 9 years, he still wanted to spend the rest of his life with me. After the tears stopped, I said yes! This man had to be God sent, because most men would have walked away. He wasn't intimidated by my bossiness, but instead he knew how to shut it down when he needed to. He wasn't afraid of how I took control of certain situations, but welcomed and complemented me when I did. He wasn't jealous that he had to share me with so many other people who needed me – but knew that there was enough of me for him too. I helped him in areas where he was weak and he strengthened me where I was weak. We weren't saved, but we were good for one another. This is what I asked for and this is what God gave me. A man who loved me unconditionally, he loved his parents, he took care of his children, he didn't ask to borrow money, he paid for dinner, movies and held the car door. He wasn't perfect by any means, I wasn't perfect by any means, but we were perfect for each other. **Side Note:** I am, in no means condoning living together unmarried. In fact the bible clearly tells us not too. I'm just showing you how God, even before we knew Him intimately and had an understanding that living together was wrong, even when the world approves it – began working on us in the midst of our sin. Now that you know, you have an obligation to live by what the bible says...not by what the worlds says.

When we returned home I was as happy as a pig in slop. I survived a heart attack and gained a fiancé all in one week. But the storm wasn't over. Two days after returning home, I had to be rushed back into the hospital. The leg where they performed the catheter was throbbing and I could barely walk. I went to see my cardiologist and he ran several test and concluded that I had an arterial aneurysm (the artery in my groin area where they conducted the catheter had ruptured). This was due to excessive walking at Disney World and not taking enough car-breaks to stretch. I remained in the hospital for several days until they ruled out that theory. I had simply overdone it and my body wasn't happy. I learned a very painful lesson and took it easy after that. Plus, I had a wedding to plan so I had to make sure that my health was right. I believe this is when I started easing up on going out. I was never a big drinker and didn't smoke or do drugs, but I just loved to party. This was my eye-opening moment when I wanted to take it easy. I still loved to go out and hang out – I just didn't do it as much.

My neighbors were taking a toll on me. I lived next door to some real life party-animals. They woke up partying and went to bed...wait, no – they never slept except for when they fell asleep in the driveway with their car windows down and music blaring as loud as it could – EVERY NIGHT at

2am. Back then, if I could have planned to have someone steal their car without me being ratted out, I would have. Did I mention that my bedroom window was under their driveway? So yes, EVERY NIGHT I was woken up by loud rap music, and the neighbors would be so high and drunk that we would literally stand outside and bang on their car window and they wouldn't wake up. So Akron Police Department became my best friends and my neighbor's worst enemy. All they had to do was go in the house in sleep. By mid-year we had had enough and decided to buy a house and we moved far away from the nonsense. I had enough drama going on inside my home that the last thing I needed was added drama outside my home too, especially with my neighbors.

By the fall of that year we had purchased a house and began planning for our future as Mr. and Mrs. June of 2006 we said our vows and I can honestly say that everything that I had endured and went through up to that point no longer mattered. I was about to walk down the aisle into the arms of the man that God sent to me. The bible tells us "He that <u>finds</u> a wife finds a good thing." **Ladies:** Quit looking for a man. God will send the right one to you once He's done making Him over and making you over. We are never going to be perfect, but when God sends him, he will be perfect for you. And God had sent this man who had accepted all my past failures, hurts, issues, insecurities, felony, bossy ways, kids and neighborhood kids. He accepted them all and I was excited to be his Mrs. I didn't look like those issues. I didn't resemble those problems. They no longer had a hold of me. They were no longer a secret. I shared my fears with this man and he still said "I Do." I shared my dreams with this man and he still accepted me for who I am. God delivered me from the initial heart attack, from the scare of a ruptured artery and sent me my Boaz! Yes indeed, I found a reason to praise Him. **#DELIVERER!** Time and time again, HE delivered me from the hands of the enemy. Even when I didn't realize HIS hand on my life – HE was there. He never left me and that alone is a reason to thank HIM because I don't look like what I've been through.

Psalm 91:3-6 *(NKJV) 3 Surely He shall deliver you from the snare of the fowler[a] and from the perilous pestilence. 4 He shall cover you with His feathers, and under His wings you shall take refuge; His truth shall be your shield and buckler. 5 You shall not be afraid of the terror by night, nor of the arrow that flies by day, 6 Nor of the pestilence that walks in darkness, Nor of the destruction that lays waste at noonday.*

CHAPTER 7 - TRANSFORMATION

In 2006, we got married and were living for real as husband and wife, trying to figure out how to adjust to this new lifestyle. He was no longer my boyfriend but now my husband. I took vows to love him through good and bad and to honor and obey him, but I had no idea how to honor and obey him. This bossy, demanding spirit had taken root in my life and I had to keep reminding myself that 1) I could not talk to him any kind of way because he was now my husband; and 2) this is what I asked God for. So yeah, I still had a lot of old habits that he did not like but he chose to put up with them because he loved me. But me, I had not learned how to relinquish control. Before him, I ran my house, I raised my kids, I paid my bills, I had my own money (what little I did have). I was used to doing things my way. And after marriage, I wanted some things to remain the same. It was either my way or no way. I had not learned the meaning of compromising. I wanted it all...but only if it was my way. How do you compromise when you want everything your way? When you are used to having everything your way...even when you are dead wrong? For the most part, I got my way until he had had enough. He was stern, no backing down, but always with a loving and gentle undertone. He made sure that when he came to correct me...and it was often, that it was never with harsh words. He was truly my Boaz! Through his actions, he loving showed me how to compromise. He showed me how to trust him. He apologized even when he was right and I was wrong. He showed me how to give with no strings attached. You think we would have learned a lot of this before marriage since we were together for 10 years before saying "I do", but my focus was on <u>my</u> children, <u>my</u> family, <u>my</u>

household. Everything was "MY", until I said "I do" and then it became "OURS." I was never a selfish person, but I didn't understand the concept of compromise.

By no means am I an expert in marriages; but I can say that some thing's should be worked out before walking down the aisle. Yes, he's the perfect man for me, but we had to endure a lot of rough days, months and years after the marriage because we didn't take time out to talk and work through them beforehand. Marriage is work. And even if those things would have been talked through before we got married, there are still going to be some hurdles that come along to try to tear down what God built up. Marriage is a constant work in progress especially when you are blending two families together; and if anyone tells you differently they are lying. If it's not the kids, it is money, if it's not the money it is family, if it's not the family, it is religion...I can guarantee that it is going to be something! And trust me that something will find its way into your marriage if you stay married long enough. Some of the secret ingredients to a happy marriage are God, communication, God, sex, God, intimacy and God. And be willing to work through the issues. It is so easy to walk away but it takes work to stay and fight. We weren't living for God so we didn't know that God was supposed to be the center of our marriage...but God knew. He knew what he had ordained. He knew how our lives would end up. And He knew that He had put a fight in both of us that would cause us to push for our relationship.

There were a lot of days where I had to do a lot of self-checks. Check my mouth. Check my attitude. Check my actions. Everything about me had to have an overhaul. If I wanted my marriage to work, I had to conduct several...ongoing self-evaluations and make some serious adjustments.

SIDE NOTE LADIES: when things go wrong in our marriages it's not always the husbands fault. Sometimes we are required to step back, and look at things from a 50,000 foot lens in order for us to get a full view of the issue. It would have been easy for me to say, "you're not meeting my needs because of x, y, z" – not even realizing that my expectations were so unrealistic that even superman wouldn't have been able to meet them. It's okay to say we are wrong. It's okay to apologize. It is okay to forgive them when they are wrong, but talk about it. And when you do – move on. Don't hold on to the things that once had you bound.

I had a lot of deep rooted issues that had never been addressed and that I could not shake on my own. For years I tried blocking things out, suppressing my emotions, and being demanding, not trusting and going through the motions of just living. I was flopping around like a fish out of water and just like the woman with the issue of blood who tried everything; I too had to touch the hem of His garment (Luke 8:43-48). I touched Him and He touched me and something broke. My stony heart began to be chiseled away and I began to relinquish control. It's amazing that when God touches you for real, how quickly transformation begins to take place. I still had issues but I was no longer stuck just existing. Changes were happening in my life and for the first time <u>I loved me some me</u>. It's okay to let go and move on. It's okay to stop playing the role of the victim. It's okay if we begin to celebrate our uniqueness, our beauty and even our issues. Yes…even your issues. Because once you acknowledge that you have issues, is when God can come in and begin to do a quick work.

So I thank God for sending me my Boaz! This was a long uphill battle and I wasn't fit for my husband. But God sent him to me to show me how to love unconditionally, trust with no strings and demands attached, relinquish control, compromise and to learn how to be a better woman! I thank God for the struggle because He gave me an opportunity to meet the new me. I wasn't bitter, but God made me better. **#GODofTRANSFORMATION** I Thank God I don't look like what I've been through.

Reference: *The entire book of Ruth*

CHAPTER 8 – MY RESTORER

In June 2007, I graduated from college with two bachelor degrees. I am the first in my family (mother and father's side) to complete college and this was a huge accomplishment. A week before I completed, I was offered a nice promotion at work. I now know that God's hand and favor were upon my life. I hadn't even graduated yet and was called into a meeting with the VP of our H.R. department and was informed that they had CREATED a new position for me. For who???? For me. I worked extremely hard to get to that point and was super excited about the opportunities that lied ahead. I was working in a new field, with new people, learning lots of new stuff. What a way to start off a new career. I no longer had to penny pinch to make ends meet. I didn't believe in living over my means and having extra cash at the end of every pay check was nice.

Over the next year I took advantage to learn all that I could. I was the only black female in my department and I was making strides. Outside of work, my home life was great and my husband and I had been church hopping looking for a stable home. It was the spring of 2008 and by this time we had visited almost every church in the city and were not drawn to become a member at any of them. It wasn't because they were not anointed; it just was not where God was calling us to be. I remember my son and my grandson's mother had invited me to attend my grandson's baby dedication at the Burning Bush Church. I was definitely going so I could witness him being given back to God; but I was also curious because I had never heard of this church or the pastor. **Side Note:** When God wants to get your attention HE will send you where HE needs you to be. I remember walking in and seeing a couple of familiar faces, but not too many. The congregation was very young compared to other churches that I had visited. But more than anything else, God spoke to me that day. I don't remember ever hearing His voice before, but this day He spoke to me. I returned the following Sunday and have been a faithful member ever since. The Word of God was hitting me hard Sunday after Sunday. God was speaking to my past situations and breaking the chains off of me. Things that I thought I had overcome had just been muffled and not really dealt with and the Word had come to cleanse me. I cried so much and I didn't understand it…but I was eager to get back in the House of God Sunday after Sunday. I had been touched for real by God and couldn't wait to be back in His presence. I couldn't explain it. All I knew was that God was there and I wanted to be where He was.

At work, somewhere along the way of me learning and striving for greatness, unbeknownst to me, someone made an assumption about something I was supposedly had done and got offended; and they set off the alarm. That was a mouth full – but that's exactly how it happened. The alarm that said, "I don't like you and you have to go", "Oh, so you think you 're better than everyone else...well let's see", "go back to where you came from" and "You will never advance as long as I'm here." What had just happened? I was in the dark. I had no idea what the problem was, when it happened or why.

A very respectable, prominent leader in the organization who people looked up to was out to get me. When they spoke, people listened. They created a fictitious problem, got people to buy in on it (without proof I might add) and viola the perfect storm began. They started building a case against me and if I hadn't been the target for their assignment, I too would have easily believed it. God was quickly teaching me a lesson of how not to judge others lest ye be judged (Mathew 7:1).

The case was rock solid, so they thought. My attackers called me into a meeting and tried to strong-arm me into demoting myself into an entry level position. Now, I've never professed to be the sharpest knife in the drawer, but I knew this wasn't right. But, how do you fight someone who has all the power? How do you convince leadership that you are innocent? This person had literally gotten four other employees fired prior to picking a fight with me. I felt like I was backed into a corner and looking down the barrel of a shot gun with no way of escape. How could this be happening?

My life was going great. Home life…no problems. Church was off the hook and I was building a relationship with God. I thought my job was cool too...until now. What did all this mean? Yes, I was still a little radical and matter-of-fact at work, but my seniority allowed me freedom and flexibility. I know I didn't always follow all of the rules and really, if someone didn't like me – I didn't care. I had been there so long that I began to develop a "rude, I don't care" attitude. But this wasn't the problem. This wasn't the case they were building. Finally, it was revealed that they were complaining about my work performance. My what? Not me! My work spoke for itself. I took pride in what I did, so I made sure that things were done and completed in excellence. Now, the other charges I would have easily been guilty of...but not this. These were straight bogus charges. I faced a judge and a jury in my past life and I was guilty of all charges. However, this was different.

I found that I had to fight when I was totally innocent. This entire situation took me back to the verse in the bible "you reap what you sow" or the statement "karma, what goes around comes around." Baby listen, this came straight out of left field and it was starting to take a toll on me. I immediately took a 30 day medical leave of absence because the night sweats had started again, the anxiety attacks were non-stop and my cardiologist was afraid that I was experiencing symptoms of another heart attack.

I experienced my first mini nervous breakdown. I was going to church every Wednesday and Sunday, but yet this trivial stuff had complete control over my emotions. I remember driving to bible study one night while I was on medical leave and I cried out to God and told Him "Lord I can't do this without you. Help me." That night my pastor was preaching a 12 week series on "The Bait of Satan." And during his teaching he mentioned that even in a situation when we are right, we as believers have to go back to our accusers and apologize...especially if they believe they have been offended. God was speaking to me again. Just when I thought I was finished getting beat up on by His word, He had another message for me. **Side Note:** We serve a God of correction and the more we grow the more the Word will come to correct us.

I thought to myself – Lord, You really want me go and apologize to these people who attacked my character, who tried to get me fired and who slandered my name throughout the company? This had to be a joke. But it wasn't. I returned to work two weeks after this message and on my drive there, the Holy Spirit reminded me of this message and once again echoed, "Apologize." This was going to be the hardest thing I ever had to do. I wasn't used to apologizing, especially to people who had done me wrong. I told one of my co-workers about what God had instructed me to do, thinking that he would talk me out of it. But to my surprise he said, "well if you don't want to get whooped on any more, I advise you to do what you were instructed." I just looked at him, agreed and walked away. I went back to my desk and began talking to myself and to God. Trying to see if He changed His mind about what He told me to do. Have you ever had one of those moments? When you tried to talk God out of something He told you to do? I took a deep breath (more like 10 of them because I was still hoping God would change His mind) and when He didn't, I went in search of the person.

I called them into an office and apologized. It was quick and believe it or not, it was also sincere. I then went through the organization and apologized to everyone who I knew I had offended during my tenure there...and there were several people. I had forgotten about most of them, but when I had finished with one, the Holy Spirit would bring one more to my remembrance. All I could do was chuckle and be obedient. And to be truthful, most were shocked that I was apologizing (and so was I); however all were receptive and appreciative. I guess there's no denying the power of the Holy Spirit. When He speaks, not when I speak, but when HE speaks, people will listen.

As I look back on this season, I realize that out of everything I had experienced in life (rape, abortion, jail, almost dying, used by men, losing a brother and so on) – God used my job, of all things, to humble me. A situation that was private immediately became public. My character and name were slandered. My reputation was drug through the mud and this began my journey of being broken and humbled.

After I apologized to all of my co-workers, I had previously scheduled meeting on my calendar to attend. The invite was from our H.R. department and was sent before I returned to work. I had no idea what the agenda was. All I was told was "go to the meeting and if you are not satisfied with the outcome, come and see me." I assumed that the meeting was to resolve all of the open "issues" before I left on medical leave; and this was my one way ticket out the door. To much of my surprise, during the meeting, I was informed that I would be reporting to someone different. I had been assigned a mentor whose goal was to coach me and help me get to the next level and I was also given a raise. All of this happened within 30 days while I was out on medical leave. Little did I know, while God was working on me, He was also making provisions on my job. I can only imagine how the situation would have turned out if I had not been obedient to God's instructions. I went from being on the verge of being fired to receiving a raise and a mentor. I went from having a nervous breakdown to being restored. I learned what humbleness was and what it wasn't; and I learned all it God's way. I was broken, but in the Potters Hands, He who was able to put me back together.

I often tell people you should humble yourself, because if God has to, it's not going to easy. I thank Him for creating in me a clean heart and renewing a right spirit within me. I praise God this situation didn't make me bitter, but made me better. **#HeRestoredMe** and I thank God I don't look like what I've been through.

Psalm 51:10-12: *10 create in me a clean heart, O God; and renew a right spirit within me.* 11Cast me not away from thy presence; and take not thy holy spirit from me. 12Restore unto me the joy of thy salvation; and uphold me [with thy] free spirit.

CHAPTER 9 – LOVER OF MY SOUL

The year is 2010 and things are going great. My new mentor was God sent. She went over and above her assignment and really took me under her wing. Keep in mind that my corporate experience wasn't the same as most peoples. Most people had the teaching and molding from their parents, graduated from high school and then on to college...my journey wasn't the same. What I should have learned at 21 years old, I was just learning at 42. I was behind on the learning curve and had a lot of catching up to do. I was eager to learn on and off the job.

I had been at my church for two years now and was simply enjoying being in the atmosphere of praise and worship every week. I saw God move week after week. People were being delivered. Speaking in tongues and my desire to be filled with the Holy Spirit was growing daily. I noticed that God was calling me to pray almost every night and I enjoyed sitting at His feet getting fed. None of the prayers were for me. In fact, I don't remember praying much for myself but always for someone else. I didn't mind, I just wanted to be obedient in the sight of God. My relationship with Him was growing. I didn't quite understand most of what was happening in my life, but I enjoyed it. I was eager to do more because I wanted more.

I remember tarrying one night with the Burning Bush mid-wives (this is what I call them), seeking to be filled with the Holy Spirit. Two ladies, that are gifted in creating an atmosphere where the Holy Spirit can dwell. I didn't get filled that night and I later found out it was because I was afraid. I wanted to predict and control the moment instead of letting God do what He does best. I know God to be a gentleman and He will not enter an unwilling vessel that's scared and has guards up. He wants us to want Him as much as He desires for us to be right in His sight. It took me a while to understand that and I thank Him for teaching me how to love and welcome Him. I spent all of 2010 and most part of 2011 getting to know Him in a more intimate way. The head of my life, the lover of my soul and my beginning and my end. And As I loved on Him even more – one tragedy after another hit my family. God strategically drew me closer to Him because He knew these situations were coming to challenge my faith. And if I had not experienced Him wrapping me in His arms and drawing me closer, I would have lost everything. My uncle died of cancer in January, someone tried to kill my son, my mother-in-law died in July, someone burned down our family home in October and almost killed my mother and then someone successfully murdered my son in December. In twelve months, **I went from being on top of the world to the world being on top of me.** All the while, the Holy Spirit had me wrapped in His loving arms. I didn't know it until the storm was over. But just like I tell my children, if God created a storm, you better believe that He will also provide an umbrella for shelter. Just like in a natural sense, each spiritual storm has a category associated with it.

- Jan 2011 - My uncle's death was a category 1 storm where I was able to run through it without any covering. But learned that I needed a little more protection.
- Jun 2011 - Someone trying to kill me son was a category 2 storm where I needed a light poncho. In the natural sense, stage 2 is categorized to

produce light damage; and it did. It had the family on pins and needles but we got through it and I knew it was by God's grace and mercy that he lived.

- Jul 2011 - My mother-in-law dying was a category 3 storm (heavy rain and wind moving at 85 miles per hour). This level is understood to produce significant damage. My mother-in-law's passing created a void, emptiness and loneliness in my husband's family. Basic covering would not suffice. I needed to tap into some spiritual covering and increase my faith and prayer life.

- Oct 2011 - My mother's house being burned down and her being caught in the fire, was a category 4 storm like a hurricane; and I had to take full cover and caution. This level is noted to be catastrophic to humans, structures and property. Un-repairable damage and destruction was done. We lost almost everything...but her life was spared. We experienced betrayal, loss of possessions and I fell into a depression.

- Dec 2011 - My son being murdered – was a full blown Tsunami and was declared a state emergency. I lost my MND!

I needed God to step in and provide some shelter from these storms. Every few months they became worse and worse. The winds (situations) were too strong for the temporary coverings (anointing) that I was using. I learned that you cannot fight a Goliath with a seven sons of Sceva anointing (Acts 19:14-16). We have to be prepared for the storms; that's why God continuously tells us in Ephesians (6:11-18) that we must put on the whole armor of God.

With most natural disasters, each progressing storm stripped away a layer of foundation. My faith, my love, my trust, my mind and my hope. But also like every natural disaster, the best of the best are always sent in to assess the situation and provide relief (US Coast Guard, Red Cross and FEMA). In my situation – the best of the best was also sent in… THE FATHER, THE SON and THE HOLY SPIRIT. Jesus stepped in right in the nick of time and saved me from me. I was at the end of my rope. I didn't want to live, I wanted to do harm to others and I wanted my son back. But God said no. When God speaks, there's nothing else that needs to be said. He has a gentle way of checking us in the midst of our mess and sadness and shaking us back to reality. I'm thankful that I not only serve a loving God, but a God who sent people to pray for me. They prayed for me when I couldn't pray for myself. Even in the most difficult times, God was there. Even when I didn't know it or feel Him there, He was with me the entire time. Deuteronomy 31:6 reminds us to: *Be strong and courageous, do not be afraid or tremble at them, for the LORD your God is the one who goes with you. He will not fail you or forsake you.*

My son was gone, the funeral had come and gone, my faith was restored and my heart was still broken, but I knew God was still in total control. And since I had accepted Him as the head of my life, whatever decisions He made, I had to be okay with them. After all, He only created the heaven and earth and everything in between. Surely He knew what was best for me and how to fix my wounded heart.

The attacks continued to come, but I was stronger and wiser. Instead of looking to my family and friends for help, I called on the name of Jesus. The bible states it best in 2 Chronicles 20:15 that the battles are not ours but His...so Lord here you go. Here's one more battle for you to fight and deal with. My army is not big enough, but You are my protection. I don't have enough strength to fight one more battle, but you are the epitome of strength...so here you go.

I had a long road to go before I found normalcy and to be honest it wasn't easy, but much easier because I had the Holy Spirit, who is my Comforter, on my side. There were many nights that I cried but the cries didn't last long. I felt the shear presence of the Holy Spirit when I wept. There's not a soul alive that could have provided the comfort that the Holy Spirit provided. We try to be there for our loved ones, but I'm telling you there's nothing like the love and comfort of Jesus. I truly thank everyone who was there for me during my storms, but just so there's no misunderstanding...God and God alone healed me, delivered me and set me free. No man can do for me what He has done.

I praise God for being the **#LOVERofMYSOUL**. And even though these trials had the ability to destroy me, God said...not now...not on my watch. So I thank God for saving me and that I don't look like what I've been through.

CHAPTER 10 – SEASON OF SEPARATION

About a year and a half after my son's passing I found myself in the wilderness. I had been in this rut for close to eight months and could not seem to shake this feeling. It was a feeling of abandonment, loneliness, hurt and betrayal. I found myself faced with one situation after another wondering why all of a sudden I was an outcast. Trying to figure out why I no longer received invites to family functions, cookouts and gatherings. Were they afraid that I would come dressed as Mary or Martha and come quoting scriptures? I couldn't figure it out. All I know is that I went from being apart to set apart. People turned their backs on me because I serve God. But what they didn't understand is that He is the same God that rescued them from their sins when life had them bound.

People said that I had changed, and they were right. When you've had a true encounter with Jesus, there's nothing about you that can remain the same. I didn't cuss anymore. I forgave quickly and easily. And I genuinely loved on people, even if they didn't love me. The work that had begun in me was noticeable to everyone. I just loved the Lord and I wanted my family back like it used to be. I just wanted them to love me. But instead, God was showing me that He loved me. He loved me in spite of my flaws, my failures, my past issues and my insecurities. And as He began to mold me, He also began replacing their love with His unconditional Love. He loved me enough to die for me and even though my family claimed to love me, I don't believe that they would die for me. So God took me through a season where He had to show me my flaws. My flaws of putting more love, faith and trust in my friends and family, than I had in Him. My relationship with people, was more important than my relationship with God. So the separation process began. I had to learn to lean on and trust God with my full being. And when my life began to line up with the will of God, it caused confusion with those who were not aligned to His will.

They did not understand that this change they were seeing in my life was all God's doing, not mine. That I was only following the call, I did not create it. The gossip started, the insinuations began, and before I knew it there was a gap as wide as the red sea between me and those I loved. What they didn't realize was that with every harsh word they spoke or indirect bad act, it was like they were killing me spiritually and throwing dirt on my grave. And as I began to cry out to the Lord, The Holy Spirit stepped in and reminded me that I serve a God who covers and protects His own. Just when I thought I had lost the battle, the Holy Spirit directed me to the book of Ezekiel (37:1-14). And just like God spoke to Ezekiel and asked him "can these dry bones live?" Ezekiel's response was "O Lord, God thou knowest", and then God told him to prophesy to those dry bones. God also sent my Pastor, De'Juan Kelker II, and commanded him to prophesy of my dry bones. **Side Note:** God sees every tear that we cry and hears every prayer. And just when we are at our lowest point, God will send someone to speak a word to our issues. As I sat at church, in that sanctuary, week after week, and heard sermon after sermon, God's words echoed in my soul and breathed life into my dead situation. Week after week, my bones began to rattle, the scales began to fall off my eyes, my flesh became alive again and my ears were opened. I was alive again.

I remember driving home from bible study one night and I asked God, "Where were you when I was dying?" And I heard a soft voice say "I was resuscitating you." I cried and worshipped Him all the way home. And before I knew it, I was praising God for choosing me. I was praising God for bringing me through. I was praising God for thinking enough of me to call me His own. I was praising God for saving my raggedy soul. And I was reminded that THE SAME ONES WHO WITNESSED MY DEATH as they assassinated my character, talked about me and counted me out, NOW HAVE TO TESTIFY OF MY RESURRECTION! I'm alive and I'm stronger. God took me, when no one else cared and they were not looking; and cleaned me up. As they gossiped "she's a mess", HE said "she's a message." And as they look at me now, they cannot deny that they played a role in what they thought was going to be my demise, but they also have to understand that it was never God's intention that I perish.

I learned that God was teaching me how to forgive and how to love. I remember praying and I asked God to teach me how to love like Him. To give me a heart like His and to use me for His purpose. And in order for God to use me, He had create situations which required me to love in spite of. He had to change me. He had to break me. And then He had to restore me. Mathew 18:21-22 tells us we are to forgive our brother (gender neutral) 70x7 and Mathew 5:44 tells us to love your enemies and pray for those who persecute us. I've learned over the years that our enemies are not always strangers...but could possibly be those we've loved and trusted all of our lives. No matter the person or the situation, we are called to serve God and continuously love in spite of.

It took me a while to understand that some people are spiritually deaf and blind, just as I was when I was living for the world. But, I know only God can open blind eyes and deaf ears, just as He did for me. And only God can send an Ezekiel to speak to their dry bones. My role is to pray. Pray without ceasing and stand in the gap for them. Pray that they will recognize the tugging they feel and accept the call from God before it's too late. My role is to plead with them to turn from their ways and repent. To intercede for them and their salvation and love them in spite of how they treat me. Someone reminded me that if Jesus' own kind rejected Him, surely I wasn't exempt from the same treatment. And the word is clear in Mathew 10:22 *"You will be hated by everyone because of me, but the one who stands firm to the end will be saved."* So instead of being mad, hurt or revengeful – I stand firm.

People were falling by the wayside. People who I thought would be in my life forever have now become a memory that I talk and reminisce about. I love them and will continue to pray for and stand in the gap for them, but I also understand that they are not my assignment.

My assignment had been revealed and I was fighting with accepting it. However, in a sermon my pastor preached he stated "God is separating us from people so we can complete our assignments. And when your assignment is revealed, so is the enemy." Some people are total distractions and have the ability to abort our assignment just by their shear presence. So, to ensure that assignments are completed, people who could potentially threaten the completion were removed from my life…it could be for a season or a lifetime.

- I've been persecuted for serving God...count it all joy.
- I've been separated from people because of my assignment... that's a blessing.
- He snatched me out of the hands of the enemy and turned my life around...I'm winning.
- He filled me up with His precious Holy Spirit...that's staying power.
- He gave me a new language and a new heart to love His people.... I'm in awe.
- He called me to intercede for His people...what an Honor!

God is continuing to work in my life and in 2013 I was ordained as an Elder at my church. I am extremely humbled by God's hand on my life. I love the Lord and I know and understand that every trial that I endured was a part of God's plan.

I had to endure the test in order to have a testimony. We all have situations that God has brought us out of that we should be telling people about. It's not to be ashamed of, but to highlight how God had us covered the entire time and how He delivered us. We weren't ashamed to take His hand of Grace and Mercy to help us out of the situation; therefore we shouldn't be ashamed to tell people how He rescued us out of our mess.

I was raped, promiscuous, had children out of wedlock, was tore up from the floor up, was a liar, cheater, fornicator, betrayer, had a sharp tongue, cussed, partied, was headed for destruction and had accepted a life of ungodliness. But Jesus stepped in and changed my ways, my thoughts, my tongue, my heart and my life. So I praise HIM! **And I thank GOD that I don't look like what I've been through.**

CHAPTER 11 – WORDS OF ENCOURAGEMENT

Do not let "society" define who you are or are not based on your past. We serve a God who's word tells us in Haggai 2:9 that our Latter shall be Greater! God is able to open doors that no man can close and close doors that no man can open. So keep pressing and know that He is GOD all knowing. There is nothing that we can do or have done that surprises Him. Remember that He knew us before we were even formed in our mother's wombs. He just wants us to acknowledge that He is Lord. He is King. He is Alpha and Omega. He is the Great I AM and then repent. Every day we wake up we should repent because we're going to mess up somewhere along the way.

I'm not proud of the things that I've done in my past that has brought shame to God's name. Nor am I encouraging others to do wrong; I'm simply pointing out that if you made some mistakes, know that we serve a loving God, a forgiving God and a God of transformation; and HE is able to turn any situation around.

I am not who people say I am, I am who GOD says I am. He calls me fearfully and wonderfully made. I didn't beat the odds, God called me and then He took my hand and pulled me up out of the muck and mire and for that I will be forever grateful.

If you look at my past without GOD in it – it looks grim. But once I include HIM, it now becomes a testimony. The creator of all things has told me that "my later shall be greater." With all of the hell that I had to endure, if that's any indication of my future, I can't do anything but rejoice and shout Hallelujah!

So in spite of what it looks like, hold your head up and know that HE can change the impossible to possible to where you don't look like what you've been through.

Father, I come humbly before you and ask that you seek the hearts of your children. Begin to do an inside job in each one of us Lord. Open our blind eyes to see and hear you clearly. Allow us to respond to the tugging of the heart and stir up the gifts that you've birthed in each of us. Lord, your people are hurting. We need more of you and less of ourselves. Show us the straight paths to take. Show us how to be more like you. How to have a heart like you. How to love like you. Lord, let your word begin to marinate in our spirits and manifest in our lives.

Lord, begin to break the strongholds off of our lives that are holding us back from doing what you've called us to do. Sharpen our discernment and give us 20/20 vision in the spiritual realm so we can clearly see the tricks of the enemy. Give us wisdom to know Your truths. And strengthen us to continue in this spiritual warfare. In Your might name I pray, AMEN and AMEN.

ABOUT THE AUTHOR

Crystal Varner is married to her wonderful husband, Johann, of 10 years. She currently holds a BA in Marketing and a MBA. God's grace opened a door for Crystal to work in Corporate America; where she has been employed for 19 years.

She was been ordained into the office of Elder in 2013 and is striving daily to make God proud. She received an audible call from God into ministry and is studying daily to show herself approved.

Crystal also authored the book, The devil Told his Side of the Story, NOW LET ME TEL MINE. Where it walks the reader through 18 months of her life where the devil had total access to her. She was on the brink of losing her mind, her faith and her love for people, but God stepped in and restored it all. The book can be purchased on www.amazon.com.

For speaking engagements and interviews - the author can be reached at crystalvarner21@gmail.com

www.ingramcontent.com/pod-product-compliance
Lightning Source LLC
Chambersburg PA
CBHW032053150426
43194CB00006B/517